MW00612044

Black Type Poems

by
Christopher Michael

Released June 2021

Printed in the United States of America
Cover Photo Tova Charles Photography
Cover Design Christopher Michael
Edited by Sunni Soper
ISBN 978-1-7333152-4-1
Published by 310 Brown Street
www.310brownstreet.com
www.mrmichael310.com

Black Type Poems

HOOTIE BLVD 5800

HOOOOOO LA 310

Christopher Michael

POET

Christopher Michael

Black Type Poems

Children of God

I've heard,
that words don't matter.

Then why,
did God use them to make all of creation?

We poets,
merely children playing with daddy's tools.

The pen,
the deadliest of spears we cut life into paper.

The stage,
the shoes he leaves at the door we're just trying to stand in.

The mic,
his hammer heavy to lift but we keep trying.

We poets!
We gods!
We children of the Most High!

How dare you tell God how to speak?

Christopher-Michael

Black Type Poems

This is God work

Dear Poet,

As much as you make your poems about you they never will
be.

They will always be about the affect they have on the reader
or hearer be careful cause you can make the listener the
doer of your words. You are the correspondent of this
community so Speak truth and

When the father forces you to function in the favor he's fixed
you in, fantastic fortune follows and falls at your feet. Speak
and there will be a sea of similes setting at the shore of your
tongue. The almighty mother of life will move mountains of
metaphors out of your mouth in moments
you don't even know you're prepared for.

You will turn Post Traumatic Stress Disorder
into Poems That Stop Death,
cause Poets Turn Struggle into Dreams realized
Know that P T S D are just more letters for you to ladder
your way to Possibilities Transcending Suicide Domestic
violence and
People's Toxic Self Destruction.

You will be able to Mary Poppins pain and truth into a
spoonful of sugar. People will listen to you even when they
have built walls along the borders of their hearts. You will
open doors when you Shonda your Rhymes. Your writing
will Harriet Tubman someone to freedom. Your mouth will
Michelle Obama someone's backbone.

Your experience, your vision, your art, your heart will
Oprah Winfrey in front of millions. Your success will Mae C.
Jemison out of this world, gravity will not contain you but
you will Nikki Giovanni bind your words into books and
after you (fist) Angela Davis the next revolution children

7

will speak your name, study your words and recite your work.

Your voice will command attention your presence will grab the spotlight, but it will never, be
about

YOU!

So,

Don't you dare dim your pen or mute your muse for no man or woman, not the last ex or the next you are blessed. Purge your pain on page and leave it for the world to learn from your mistakes. You can't beacon in a storm if you hide your light. You don't know what hurricane the reader needs to be sheltered from, be the warning and the calm after the storm.

If life and death is in the power of the tongue then you, you, brilliant human are a weaponized wordsmith with a velvet voice.

If god spoke the universe into existence, then you are an architect, construction worker, a bulldozer, a wrecking ball, a jackhammer, a glue gun, a cement mixer, a bricklayer, a needle and thread, a gardener, a god in the earth and you can manifest anything that you can shape with your mouth, but do not take this power lightly. The tongue is a double-edged sword more dangerous than Excalibur, the sword of omens, a blazing sword, a spear in the side of a messiah, a fat man, a little boy, a badge and a gun, an infinity gauntlet or any other fantastic weapon the human mind can manifest, fact or fantasy.

But this be a burden. So Before you dabble in this art know that creation is god work and true poets wield words with the weight of the universe.

Now go write something, POET! I dare you.

~Christopher Michael

9

This Book Contains the Following Type of Poems

Lecture Type Poems

Emotional Type Poems

Sexy Type Poems

more Sexy Type Poems

Black Type Poems

Reflective Type Poems

Christopher Michael

Black Type Poems

Why Do you Write?

Artist: I write in an attempt to encapsulate the embodiment of a cultured pain while painting the victim into victor, assessing world views of self through nature and mechanics allowing the reader to open themselves up to a change process synesthetically reading the smell, hearing the colors, and tasting a truth butterfly transformation of their thought process.

Christopher Michael: I put this word with that word and it sounded good.

Black Type Poems

Lecture Type Haiku

Whether or not you
are a king or a pawn, You
are still getting played.

Your breath stinks cause you
talk shit about everyone.
try encourage-mints

Lecture Type Poems

Black Type Poems

They'll Make Your Grass Green with Envy

When Intelligence and familiarity make love, they breed contempt. They get a dog named persecution, always sniffing up the ass and biting the hand of prosperity. They love your lawn walking past what you built pretending not to notice, imagining every back they could bury your beautiful blades of grass in.

Something about doing better that poisons people's perception. They'll be so pissed off it feels like being pissed on (it's not rain). They'll try to subtly suggest you away from significance. They'll project their inadequacies, anxieties and failures on you. Hands so full of doubt they can't see their own wings. Self-loathing so loud they can't hear you teaching them how to climb and fly.

They'll try to pull you down, grabbing your ankle to get their own lift before you get a chance to anchor yourself at the summit as if they dread that come dawn, you won't return with a helping hand to ray of sunshine illuminate the path.

Maybe it's the fear of being abandoned to their own initiative, determination and luck that has them quick to lynch <u>your</u> better with the rope you lowered to help them. They'll Columbus your accomplishments like they discovered you. When you offer resistance, they return with fire water, boom sticks, tainted blankets and an invitation to a trail of tears and offer no tissue while they try to wipe you out.

Mediocrity will honor achievement with resentment. If only they could get full off the envy that eats away at a soul already rotten and empty. You'll give them a fish for today, try to teach to fish for tomorrow and they'll hock a loogie spit disrespect in your face, wash it off when they waterboard you for all your secrets or just throw you out the boat in <u>disgust</u> that you didn't bait hook, net cast, catch, fillet, season and sear them to their own success. If

19

you don't make them the whole plate or give them what's
on your plate, they'll lemon wedge your name and sour-
word your reputation.

Haiku:
They will shit on you.
That will make your grass greener.
They'll get mad at that. (They'll hate you for that.)

I guess that means you're doing something right so step
light.
Move in silence and only share with those who celebrate
your growth with a loving push towards greatness.

Hang with those who have.

Humble yourself at the feet of,
and learn from,
those who have more.

Now go forth
and be
extraordinary.

You got people to piss off.

Some people have bad necks
so it hurts to look up and
see you at the top.

When We Were Young & Dumb & Full of...

I thought I heard him ask, "when did they begin to desire
the pussy over the person?" Learn to Love the lust over
love.

I think,
it was at the moment
puberty punctuated the hormones that triggered primal
urges
and no one was there to usher them into manhood.

We should ask:
Was there anyone there to properly educate them to the
road of understanding the power they possess?
Is it because all they had were peers placating and
pacifying the pulsating pleas of their own penis?
Fighting foreign feelings of temptation
Monday thru Sunday,
Every day is cum day
Even god's birthday
Especially Columbus day
Itching for some crotch to colonize.

Perhaps kids collect coochie like cards
cause it's the only example of control and conquest
they had to curate from.

Did anyone teach them she is not a possession to be
pocketed,
plastic sleeved
and traded
and that the only thing they own
is their choices?

To the boys, budding men and men who skipped boyhood
and went straight to daddy or dog

Son,
You are not broken.
You are not evil.
Your body is not a temple of sin and self-loathing,
you are growing.
Your body is preparing you for the role it believes you want
to walk in.
If making more people didn't feel so damn good
no one would be dumb enough to do it.

What one calls lust
another can call genetic imperative.

Propagation of the species is not a recommendation,
it's a command!
Before you're old enough to think straight your body is
making demands.

Developing minds struggling with
Body, bang.
Bible, abstain.
Community, ashamed.

Being a virgin
is of no importance if you're not the best version
of yourself.

To the community of men who daily manage their body and
minds it's time to teach and reach. Repair the breach
between us and the women that support us.

Let's learn them lust vs love and how to aim.
Teach them all of the glory and destruction that cums
through them.
How release can free you from the voices that call for
attention
or release can bind you to another human for the rest of
your life
or release can decrease your lifeline
unlocking plagues that prey on those who knock on the
doors of carnal pleasure.

22

Sex is a treasure.
Enjoy it.
But let us learn them how to connect, care, control and
cum, to mature choices.

Wish you could read this as a response to Nate Sr's "Sex Education"

23

Black Type Poems

DICK PIC (& The Truth)

A poem by some random literary genius on Facebook.
Corrected by Christopher Michael

Girl I sent you my dick

Because I'm too small to just say HI

Why do you not reply

Do you think you can ignore me like my father or something?

Are you lesbian or something

You're contributing to my feelings of inadequacy and nothing

I'm just trying to understand why

Don't you want a guy

I'm convinced this dick will improve your life

Girl I sent you my dick

Why ain't you rushing round

While you're busy building self esteem

I'm ready and waiting

To give your pussy a good pound

Ok maybe an ounce but It'll be good

Girl I sent you my dick

Ok don't reply then you hoe

25

Now you get to see how I deal with rejection

You're ugly anyways

Ugly like my attitude

Ugly like my feelings for women

Ugly like my relationships

Ugly like my inability to emotionally grow

Just thought that you should know

Poem by david w.
Improved by Christopher Michael

the b(L)ackbone

The backbone is a major part of the structural support system and protects the core of the nervous system. Is that not a Black woman? Lifting and protecting our feelings daily, not seen, not credited? When it goes out or gives up the whole-body collapses. All limbs lead to the spine. Fists can't fight, hugs can't happen without arms anchored to reliability. Is it not the backbone that lifts up the head? Is not the man supposed to be the head? While head is haughty in its overstanding the backbone is under, standing, everything!

Black Type Poems

King Be

To be king is to carry crown,
crown be weight of world
burden be broad on back,
Believe,
bring best or bear backbone breaking

King be command,
be control,
be conquer.

Like love is greatest command.
Like King loves queen,
loves lineage,
loves neighbors,
loves community,
loves legacy.

King controls destiny,
directs self into success.
King carries kingdom,
curates accomplishment.

King conquers fears
honors horror even when fear resides inside.
Fear has not the strength to restrain or obstacle him from
tasks.

King can't coronate self.
Birthright don't make right
King sees wrong
makes right
King vision lit
by god's light

Christopher Michael

Black Type Poems

Church Folks

Church folks be the biggest heathens
Elevating themselves above the people
Standing on stacks of bibles
instead of standing on the word.

Black Type Poems

Superfriends

To my social justice warriors:

On the occasion of Superman's 40th birthday his Super Friends celebrated with an all SUPER Star gala event held at the Hall of Justice. Everyone was there The Flash, Vixen, Green Lantern, Zantana, Cyborg , Selena Kyle, Jimmy Olson and Lois Lane.

It was gift opening time and the cowl covered countenance of the bat with black paint to hide his blushing eyes was saving the best for last.

Batman reached into his utility belt and revealed an Nth metal linked necklace with a beautiful emerald colored jewel encrusted pendant shaped like hope, like the emblem emblazoned on Kal-El's Chest. The jewels were so rare it took 5 years to find enough of the unearthly rock so Superman could rock this green ice. With a smile so wide with pride the Joker would laugh, but still be jealous inside, Batman lynches the necklace of good intentions around Superman's neck oblivious to the offense that would ensue.

Apparently too weak to speak for himself, Lois jumps in and says, "He shouldn't have to explain to you what he's sensitive to. That's what google's for."

Batman stands shooketh, "I was just trying to be a good friend. I saw nothing on the internet about Superman's historical sensitivity to this particular item."

And this is why allies to our cause need to know what the phuq is going on.

Of course they can do some research and Granted YOU don't owe anyone an explanation of you or access to you but you can't expect them to understand you if you don't, won't lead them! They can try and digest the contents of a

33

book or some crap-filled, over-opinionated hack ass article, but nothing conveys the truth of your story like your mouth, your eyes, your words and no one is going to be more receptive than someone who doesn't get it, but loves you enough to want to know how it makes you feel.

So, if you're tired of educating the masses to your story then maybe you've been woke for too long and now you need a nap. Lack of sleep can lead to psychosis. You should google that, then step aside and let another justice warrior pick up the banner of educating the next squad of good intentioned ready to put in the work open to change and understanding allies.

We need help, in the board rooms, back rooms, golf courses and dinner tables that still won't welcome us. Still ain't figured out that the color of our skin or the way we love makes us no less deserving of God's grace and the equality their precious paper has promised.

Don't be Batman, cloaked in the shadows of ignorance. Don't be Superman, not everyone can reach you where you're at. And don't be Lois Lane, the self-appointed attention-seeking internet activist gatekeeping wolf disguised as ally.

Be, a Superfriend.

Butterfly Bandits

There's a war of words being waged by insects, very small creepy crawly things and lizards sliding on their bellies. Among them are butterflies bombarding the borders with... bullshit but butterflies have no business babbling on the battlefield, that's why they're born, I mean morph into little more than majestic moths without a mouth unable to eat on their own they sip life through a straw.

Butterflies belong on flowers and in the stomachs of awe struck lovers but you are buried deep in my business and it's making me sick. If only I could expel you with one good shit. Maybe some milk of magnesia and a priest can help exorcise this demon out of my stomach... I mean my business. I won't say boo to you without a tape recorder and a witness.

I wouldn't trust you with the time if I was on my way to see God and I thought I might be late. I'm desperately dodging the line but you're pushing me in to hate. From confidant to contaminate a reminder of mistakes, no need to write poems about scorpions and snakes.

The world needs to know about you. Attention! Achtung! Cuidad! Attenzione!! Butterflies are dangerous too!!

Despite the warnings, I let you befriend me and here i thought I was my own worst enemy. You use gossip like grenades you're a verbal war machine mistakenly morphed into a moth, dark, dirty and flying in circles around the light of everyone else's life. Unable to generate your own you've made yourself a shadow on the wall an absence of light devoid of substance. Weighed down by evil and hate your wings can't take the strain. Too short to reach for the stars so you stand on other's pain.

Lesson learned show no loyalty, you'll earn no loyalty... That's why all your hidden words make their way back to me.

35

I won't hide my flame; I'll burn brighter from cigarette lighter to the winning game Bonfire. Come a little closer let me singe your wings. The mouth of a butterfly is more damaging than the venom of creepy crawly things.

Chained Tongue

At some point during a conversation, I said some common Spanish phrase that has long been adopted into the American-English lexicon. That's when this individual looked at me with all the seriousness of an adolescent searching for a platform to struggle on thinking they had found it in my mouth only to retort with their perfect Amero-Texas English accent "Don't appropriate my language." As if it was appropriate to talk to me like that.

Completely ignoring the lack of respect owed an elder double their years.

I laughed. I laughed so loud... on the inside. Didn't want to break this poor Child's heart, crushed by the rebuff of an adult in front of their peers.

They, a mixture of indigenous and African people, a complete concoction of colonized flesh. My view not vexed, I venerated the value of multiple vernaculars acknowledging they'd done more than me, mastering two different dialects from two different conquers. I failed Spanish in high school and English in college.

With the utmost respect I responded.

Both your languages are a reflection of the master's chains, tying your tongue and wiping the taste of your culture out your mouth. As if Columbus is any less present in your saliva forgetting that he be the Spaniard who sails across your teeth every time you speak.

The audacity of your audaciousness! You chatter as if your utterance of bovine fecal matter is not culturally tainted like both of the dictionaries you use. It's cute how you take ownership of what your people's owners shipped to their shores. Wrapping yourself around the tormentor's flag jammed down your throat. The same tyrants who stole your gold as they staked their claim with the claim of

37

escaping tyranny. While you try to Spanish inquisition my mouth you sad little crusader.

I see the line of the oppressor crackling in the creases of your frown. You are on your way to blossoming from the seeds they have planted in you. I hope you never find a struggle. I hope you never find the pain you are looking for. I hope you never grow tall enough to die on the cross you are begging to be heard from.

Regarde ta bouche quand tu me parles
Cuida tu boca cuando me hablas
Watch your mouth when you talk to me
no matter what language.

Inspired by Azeezat in Club House

What inspires you to write?

Artist: The ability to reach others with a collection of symbols that convey thoughts and ideas is a magic that has a special fascination. To change a mind or reach a heart for the betterment of a world in desperate need of love is a life's fulfillment that anyone should be honored to attempt let alone achieve.

Christopher Michael: I like the attention and sometimes the money.

Black Type Poems

Emotional Type Haiku

She my sweet potato
He stole her from me
That damn yam burgalar
(I'll spell it how I want to!)

Metrosexual feline
Blossoms up through concrete that's
a dandy lion

We made beautiful music together
fueled by our love
for baked beans

Christopher Michael

Black Type Poems

Emotional Type Poems

Black Type Poems

Prove You Love Me

When a soldier spends their days waiting, training anticipating the next fire fight it's hard to come home and relax. Being good at your job means skilled at going zero to one hundred in five seconds flat but that doesn't work when home is a city street, posted speed limits caution children playing.

When a police officer has a twenty-year career protecting the city, so we don't see the worst humanity has to offer, retirement feels like death. The quiet creeps in and you remember EVERYTHING... and miss it.

You can only live on the edge so long before edge feels normal, when your hands find home in gripping the side of the cliff face. When you've evolved to walk on eggshells, a clean floor feels like an empty house.

This is no different than years of slugging through toxic pools and deadly chemical vats then suddenly BOOM a normal boring ass healthy loving relationship. Like WTF am I supposed to do with this? How do I know this is love if there's no passion, crime scene splattered on the walls or broken hearts shattered on the floor to step on? No blood, no love.

How do I know she really gives a damn if the jealousy don't push her to check my phone, or tap my phone? How can she possibly care if her constant questioning doesn't make me hyper aware? You know how you know teachers care? You know how you know they want you to be better? Because they test you. How can she love me if she isn't always quizzing my character, trying me, poking me, pushing me?

She shouts words of encouragement to me like:
"If you hit me back, you a punk ass bitch!" or
"You just gone stand there and not hit me back you a weak ass bitch?" or

"I dare you to hit me back, stop being a bitch!"

Begging me to probe the limits of my masculinity/humanity to see how long I can last before meeting the me that values my physical security more than the rest of me, values she. I tried to get away and she hits me again!

For too many years I was a NASA test pilot and now the next one expects me to be satisfied driving a station wagon in the slow lane. Drama free, has all the exciting flavor satisfaction of sugar free. Prove you love me as much as she did. Let's fight about something. Chastise me up against the ropes. Accuse me into doing something just to prove you right! Make me scared to sleep next to you at night, so I know you phuqing care.

How can we have all the that love and passion if you keep bringing this peace? Like, WTF am I supposed to do with this?

Toppled Tower

Recovering from relationships
that tried to remak me
replacing my pieces
like a jenga tower
as if my pieces aren't already
perfectly placed
Only to fall
through their well meaning hands
a toppled tower
no help no 911

Christopher Michael

Black Type Poems

Me the Starship

I want to apologize for not falling in love with you.
I wanted to give you my heart but it's not right to give you
something that belongs to someone else.
Which explains why I feel so numb and seem so cold.
I try not to hug you too much for fear that the jagged
shards of what's left of my broken heart will hurt you.

I've been commanding this star ship since the urge to
ignite my thrusters overtook my will to fight it.
Since then, I've been hopping from station to station just
hoping for the next worm hole penetration.
Preferring to dock with space stations
cause it's hard to escape the gravity of a good planet and
I'm scared to fall in.

Keep your distance from stars,
lesson learned:
something that hot
is likely to burn.

Christopher Michael

Black Type Poems

Alien Type Love

Sometimes love is a hole you fall into.
Seemingly no escape;
having no idea where it came from.

Sometimes love walks up behind
taps you on the shoulder,
says hello
and offers you a hand.

Sometimes,
love is like walking through the bowels of an alien
spaceship. You see something worth investigating
and poke it with a stick.

It opens,
before you know it
love is wrapped around your face
eight fingers squeezing your head
tail wrapped around your throat
taking your breath away. Forcing its way into your mouth
and depositing itself in your belly.

It holds you for a little while
can't see a damn thing
love wrapped around your face
squeezing all that joy down your throat.

Then things calm down;
the initial tingling wanes
the squeeze subsides
and loves face hugger falls away
now Love is just commonplace, again.

Every once in a while,
you feel the larvae
in your belly birthing a blossoming butterfly.
They don't stay there long.

51

One day,
without warning,
love bursts through your chest,
screams for joy
leaving you a limp empty husk,
and runs off

Looking
for a new host
to infect.

...of course she mattered

I once told a woman she mattered.

It was not what she wanted to hear. It was not the acceptable phrasing of affection that society suggests is best and now her pen finds the frailty of my phrasing to be a battle cry reminding me that I'm just another shitty guy.

When I say she matters what I mean is.

She Matters like noun, physical substance, like the substance of her coco chocolate killer curves, Cheshire grin and hypnotic melt me all damn day Jell-O my spine with her eyes.

When I say we matter I mean like noun, an affair, or situation, the circumstance we have been bouncing back and forth in for longer than we have let the world know. Maybe we should be less concerned about our autumn summer relationship since all the seasons in Texas blur together anyway.

When I say she matters I mean like noun, the reason for distress or problem. Like how I told her punctuality feels like love to me, but she can't love that way. I sit distressed that I'm not in the same room with her, when she promised this is the time I'll get to be in the same room with her. It feels like I'm not enough for her to 20/20 vision on long enough to remember we had a date that day and all the other dates it's almost like Late is her middle name yet, she still matters to me.

She matters to me like she lies about her feelings or doesn't understand her feelings, hides her feelings and expects me to know exactly what she's feeling. I was only supposed to be a cuddle companion. Her friends and family only ever see her offer me the side shoulder church hug and there there back pat, she dodges kisses like politicians dodging

Christopher Michael

reporters but I'm supposed to know how she feels or comprehend what she wants and yet I keep coming back for more because she matters... to me.

When I say she matters what I mean is
She matters like scripture, First Corinthians thirteen; four, five and six and seven and eight. She makes me patient and kind. I do not envy or boast, she liquifies my pride so it's easier to swallow. I don't worry about self, she makes it hard to be angry, I don't record her wrongs but it's hard to forget the stove is hot. I hope, I endure, I believe, I bear even when, what she bore did not belong to me.

When I say she matters what I mean is
She matters like verb, be of importance; have significance, consequence, note, she carries weight. She is gravity, she pulls me in, she takes me off course, she sways me, my heart, my thoughts. Her presence in my space brings peace extinguishing my well-earned ire. She matters like verb; she influences my feelings.
When I say she matters what I mean is,
I love her.

Maybe she can't understand that.

Maybe we don't speak the same language.

I Can Love You Past Your Breath

The strength of your presence is overwhelming me
it's telling me, something is wrong.
The years of neglect have been far too long
The mere thought of being next to you brings tears to my
eye
and I don't know if we can get any closer but damnit girl
I'm gonna try
If the true test is to take the time to explore your emotional
depth
then girl,
I can love you past your breath.

I can love you past the point where weaker men pass out
I'll show you love without a doubt
I will be that M&M that refuses to melt in your mouth.
When your tongue is praying for eviction
I can move past the nasal affliction
I'll show you the true meaning of affection
Despite the fact that your toothbrush bristles are bent in
four different directions
Correction
Six different directions
I got god on my side so there's nothing you can say
to chase me away
Lean on me when you're weak cause I'm curiously strong
Like Mentos I'm your fresh maker,
Your cherry life saver
Your winter green breath saver
Like a 2-liter bottle of scope
I'll show you a world filled with hope
Tell me what you need girl I promise I won't choke
Cause I can love you past your breath

I'm man enough to pay the cost
I'll be your Teflon dental floss
It's not your fault that halitosis is a sickness
As god is my witness
I can love the fire breathing dragon in you my dear

55

Where other brothers have closed their ears in fear of the
heat you bear, I'll be there,
When your soul needs to bear witness I'll be your dental
hygienist your swish spit and rinse, the gates of hell I'll
kiss this for you, my brimstone princess
Cause I can love you past your breath

It's as if your breath is the inevitable result of the bovine
fecal matter you've been forced to swallow, from fast
talking boys with words that are hollow taking you through
the gates of hell and that weren't even worthy to follow and
with every kiss you swallow the shit they spit

But I'm gone be your breath strip
Your family pack of double mint
Every Godzilla needs a Tokyo
don't worry about my nose hairs
they'll grow back
Your words are nothing to flinch at,
I swear I'll never step back
I'll always be that
Hand full of Tic-Tacs

Together we'll get past the hurt
I'll be your packet of certs
Come gargle with me I'm your Listerine
Your one two three sticks of Dentyne
What I mean

Till we depart at the dawning of the day of our death
Baby girl
I can love you past your breath

Smile for Shannon

No matter how high the expectations of the dreams you seek. Sometimes daughters dive too deep and sometimes mothers don't awake from their sleep. Sooner or later it's your turn to weep.

Enjoy every moment like it's your last. Let go the burdens of the past. You may need to move fast, they'll only weigh you down and there's too much to do so...

Every smile I smiled today was for you. 4560 smiles an hour. That's roughly about how many times my heart beats cause every heartbeat is a smile from God.

Every breath is another chance and I would give you all my chances if they could have just taken you off that machine for a moment or two, I would breathe for you.

Cause life doesn't have right click, edit, undo I offer you 1200 opportunities an hour to just stop and smell a flower or enjoy the scent of your mother, father, child, your woman or your man.

Every breath is a chance, 28,800 moments in a day to remember the best things in life. Every breath is another opportunity to fight. Reverse your wrongs and make them right like, inhale life exhale an apology. It's something we all should do. Inhale life, exhale I Love You.

And every time you wink or blink it's a refreshing of the eye so you can enjoy God's light like, the reflection of a smile or the pride from your mother's eyes sunrise and sunsets.

So... for those of you who will never wake up and breathe in earth's light, ALL my smiles are for you.

57

Black Type Poems

BOOM (a damn happy poem)

Apparently, I don't have enough substance in my art
that relays the joy of my heart
or conveys my contentment
so I captured it
in the curves
and straight lines of these words.

I know how to be happy, but I don't have to brag about it.
What kind of life would I have with no happy, who could
live without it?

Here's my happy piece.

Happy, exuberant, intoxicated, floating, smiling from the
inside, my chest warm and full as if it used to be tight, and
cold, things just feel right, burden light. Wind filled sails of
a kite like sing songy rhyming words all night, that cheesy
smile happy. That BOOM!!   **BOOM**!!!

I might have to acknowledge to myself that I'm just too
damn happy to write this.

Let me clarify what I mean by boom. When I say boom I
mean like the first time something said let there be light
and the breaking silence triggered a universe (inspired a
universe). Like when everything is created and expands at
the same instant.

When I say happy what I mean is an overt feeling of
contentment,
so all-consuming I wanna share it with everyone
but I don't
Cause I don't want to annoy my friends,
so I hum instead
I keep it in my head

When I say friends,
I mean the people who show up for me.

59

Christopher Michael

The ones who never have excuses they just do.
They're the people I know
 I can pick up the phone
and call
and the only question is
what do you need?
Where do you need me?
They pick me up when I fall.

When I say me
I mean all the things attached to my person.

Who's your favorite poet?

Artist: I've studied the works of Maya Angelou, Langston Hughes, James Baldwin, Nikki Giovanni, Emily Dickinson, Edgar Allan Poe and Jane Marie Alejandro. I can't really put a finger on my favorite, but collectively they have shaped my work and blazed a path that I am honored to travel. We walk in the shadow of giants hoping one day they will allow us to sit upon their shoulders that we may one day grasp the stars we are reaching for.

Christopher Michael: huh? Um... Will Smith, Heavy D, Outkast and De La Soul.

Black Type Poems

(not so)
Sexy Type Haiku

Mouth tastes like last night
My finger smells like last night
man I love chicken

If we spend the night
on our backs and knees, is that
still a one-night stand?

Tried to impress her
She laughed harder than my dick
It's the funny bone

Christopher Michael

Black Type Poems

Sexy Type Poems

Christopher Michael

Black Type Poems

From A Distance

It's not my fault that the first thing I noticed is how aesthetically attractive you are. Not flawless, but a perfect picturesque combination of everything I personally identify as visually pleasing, sexy. By sexy I mean it didn't take long for me to imagine us wrapped up in an embrace for the purpose of calling forth a physical expression of the love I hoped we'd might fall into.

Maybe if you had been the service agent when I called to have my cable connected I would have noticed how soothing your voice is, how uplifting, inviting and encouraging it could be. Maybe then, by the end of the second sentence, I would have noticed how intelligent you are.

But that's not what happened.

Maybe if you had hugged me first, I would have detected how warm your spirit could be, experienced the healing embrace of your empathy. Or maybe I would have filed charges for assaulting me and violating my space cause damn. You hugging me and I ain't even seen you before is creepy. Don't do that. Consent.

But that's not what happened.

I saw you first. The particles of light that bounce off your atoms are now my favorite rays of anything. Better than Sting Rays reflecting in Ray Bans on Ray Charles singing about sweet Georgia. I bet you are the vision he imagines when he, Stevie Wonders what Georgia looks like, *A Song in the Key of Life*, you are on my mind.

I wish I could have filled my hands with you, spread the pages of your published work, thumbed through your thoughts, caressed your words with my lips, moistened my mouth with your art, fingered your feelings to first fall for

67

your substance but that's not the circumstance connection of this instance.

Sooo... Until I figure out something intelligent to say and approach with more than just player plots plans and intentions, I'll admire from a distance.

Say My Name

I love the way it passes over your lips
always amazed it even fits.

No rush, you just let it rest
As if everyone of your taste buds is putting it to the test.

I know it's long I know it's a mouthful, but your expert
tongue dances around like it studied Juilliard. I want to be
your Captive audience. You've made it the bird that sings
in your cage. You are my favorite stage. Your estuary
entertains, you have my devotion.

Your eyes say you're taking your time with it
I love how you let it sit
Lips and tongue manipulate all of it
a magician casting a spell

The sounds you make
are all the abracadabra you need to get my full attention.
Now I'm Waiting for the sleight of hand

I love the way my middle
mounted in your mouth manifests emotions in me
Feels like your mouth was made for me

The you take the first three,
then two
that's the one

Even when capitalized it fits.

All, six,
syllables of my name

Say my name
say my name

Christopher Michael

I love the way you say my name

All of it

Christopher Michael Brown

Girl,

what that mouth do?

One Night Stand

If we spend the whole night on our backs and knees,
is it still a one-night stand?

She was clearly one of the most beautiful members of the
African diaspora and I wanted to get to know her. Let me be
real. I'm not too sure I wanted anything more than a flickering
flame moment. Like a 100 pack of firecrackers we be lit, sizzle
dance all night, lots of noise and a little smoke and then we'd be
spent. Nothin' less.

As a mature adult I knew the risks and rewards of a one nighter.
It was not a habitual thing but something you might wanna try at
least once before you die.

I wanted to get to know her. Like the temperature of her skin
and how would it adjust pressed against mine. Would her lips
be as soft and smooth as they advertised?

Her breasts could not be more perfect.

Her legs were mahogany brown.

They reached from the floor

and damn near to her neck.

Honey was stacked,

like the deck

against a black man

with the cops.

Christopher Michael

Black Type Poems

The scent of my beard

The scent of my beard
after you twerked across my tongue.

Smells like peace.

Smells like clarity.

Smells like a clear path to pleasure.

The scent of my beard
triggers a vague memory
of how you flesh faced my follicles
with a waterfall flow of delicate labial indulgences.

My beard still smells good
since your absence.
The scent sent my senses
into a sensual reminiscent spiral of joy.

So much better than my usual scent
with the hint of peppermint.

Christopher Michael

Black Type Poems

when the fun begins

Ladies
By the end of this poem
You'll be reaching for a panty liner
when you need to build a damn dam around that beaver.

Aight you freaky Fellas,
First make sure your hands are clean

No,
first make sure you have consent
cause consent is sexy

After you've honored the body as a whole
And your lips have paid homage to all of her
Tongue tangoed all over her

Then you gently unwrap and expose the wet void
let your mouth take hold.

Find the spot that makes her moan.
Secure your lips right there creating an airlock
as if you were a space station protecting the last woman on
earth.

Enjoy the feeling of having the most powerful creature on
the planet dancing on the tip of your tongue
let her sit there till she's done
with you or she cums
to her senses or she cums
out of her mind.
If you need a drink of water at the end of this
Brotha you did it wrong.

So, Ring the Devil's doorbell and see who answers,
Or what opens
and watch her tremble like an LA sidewalk

75

Christopher Michael

Like you just pushed the ignition and her engine revved up
Like her body's had enough
like all hell's breaking loose.

But you keep pushing till she explodes
like a Samsung battery
Reaching for towels and changing sheets
call that flattery

She'll offer up "mmmms" "aaaahs" and "oh Gods" with her
legs high in praise.
Be it your name
or her name
or the name of her god what she means is

"I appreciate this. I consent to this, please don't stop this."

Drive her crazy and
She's gonna reach for the clutch
but you keep grinding her gears
till her toes curl back desperately reaching
but she won't find the brake
the next day you'll have to say

Not tonight baby I'm tired.
After last night I'm still tongue tied.

And she will persist.
And you can't resist

You'll say, "I told you I didn't want to have sex tonight now
you got to pay.
I know it's midnight but call yo boss and tell'em you ain't
coming in today."

Let her try and figure out how you penetrate top and
bottom her body's celebrating in your mouth while you
massage breast and both nipples at the same time.

Phuq her paraplegic,
if you can afford another lawsuit.

Be like squirrels
you Dr. Watson
she Sherlock Holmes
a perfect team always finding a nut.

Side note:
A woman once asked me what I called my manhood.
I said, Well the first 6 inches I named the tip.
I doubt if you get to meet the rest.

Sir!!!
No matter how wet she gets and the flames get higher,
put that weave to the test.
Pull In case of fire.

Don't panic if either of you thinks you see god
or the universe anew.
Let the rhythm of your mouth be her melody,
she be your heaven let her rain down on you.

Brotha put yo soul in it.
Have her scared to leave the house cause orgasms are
going viral like a global cumdemic.

My Man...

When you're done you can say with clarity
"this ass is mine".
But first Take her breath away
like COVID 69

77

Ladies, the goal is to make you sing.
While he plucks your strings
with pelvic swings
till your Nuvaring
becomes his cock ring.

And that...

is when the fun begins.

Blessed and Highly Flavored

This beauties body brought back basic brain primal responses that required a half century of conscious control. Desperately trying to remain in the bounds created by this, eyes wide open culture never taking a nap and dreaming, I was woke. But she be a living fantasy full of everything that my eyes could communicate to me that I find... interesting. The refraction of light from her frame was playing ball with my optics, I mean she was eye catching.

I have no doubts that she walks with all the authority of a self-contained soul empowered to be all she wants to be. Bet she a got a master's degree. Probably makes six figures DAMN her figure. She looks sculpted, damn near photo shopped, picture perfect. What combination of parental coupling could concoct a creature of such captivating... If she has children, I bet they honor her whole heart and move in all the success she seeks to sew, but her sexy keeps dripping on the sidewalk hope I don't slip.

I bet she owns her own business, like captain of industry. You can't walk with this much power and not be using it to legacy build. I would love to feel her self-assured security across my lips. I bet she taste like she's happy. I bet there's honey in her sweat. No damsel, no distress but this damn sundress has a fist full of my focus I mean she captured my attention. She looks Blessed and Highly Flavored. She could have my tongue if she wanted, it's hers, we could taste each other or talk. I'm dying over her walk, I just wish, it wasn't away.

Prompt from Writing and chill: Blue Lights edition "Blessed and Highly Flavored"
4th Period Poetry: Picture Prompt Poetry w/Playlist "Taste" 05.28.21

Christopher Michael

Black Type Poems

The Relationship
The Fellowship
& The Kinship

This is the story of day they left their tiny little island aboard the The Relationship, The Fellowship and The Kinship.

Imagine, bodies intertwined in a tango of touch like a torch tearing a tunnel of light into the heavens. Anchored in love, floating on desire synchronized breath fills the sails seeking passage to a new land on the vessel of relationship. Set in sunsets, all their yesterday's. Running away from others with each other fighting for the fantasy of freedom.

Time slows in the sheets. Sure that they want to reach the shore starving for arrival cannibalizing each other with mouthfuls of carnal cakes of caramelized cocoa chocolate bodies it must be magic how they are still whole. They fill holes in hearts with a whole sea of salt water. Formally fractured feelings, fixed in fleshly frames floating and fabricating a future of fortune from fountains of fornicated jubilation evidenced in the ocean of salinated joy pouring over them from eyes, lips and labia.

Winds of wonder try to blow them off the path, delirious and exhausted in the exercise of ecstasy, but they navigate each-other, eyes connect and compass back on course. Rocked back and forth, up and down these be the sexiest of storms tipping them over they spin around top to bottom, bottom back on top. Bodies clap to the rhythm of thunderclaps.

Tongues land like lightning, illuminating the dark. A tempest of temptation satiated by squalls, high and low pressure push them just past the point of pleasure to the brink of hurting so good then... winds and water stand still. The silence echoes with a faint primal drumbeat buried beneath breastbone bodies begging for breath.

81

Christopher Michael

They drift in new memories made. Steam rising from the fresh frenzy of friends finding no flaw, floating on fellowship.

Butterflies in bellies have been consumed, ravaged by rhapsody. The fog of bliss lifts and they finally cum to a new country.

They be each other's rock safely landing in open arms. Hands hold hips and hearts they rename this new land *us Untied* in a *State* of *Agreement*. The voyage has renewed their constitution and they have colonized each other with a consent that consumes them into one.

Feet firmly fixed on terra firma, arrival is not the end but the start of a legendary legacy of lust, love and life. The light in the eyes of their lineage will always give voice to the victory they have found in the journey of this kinship.

4th Period Poetry: Picture Prompt Poetry w/Playlist "Touch" 05.21.21

What art do you most identify with?

Artist: the creation of the universe, for are we all not manifestations birthed from the first spark.

CM: a preschooler's macaroni dinosaur

What jobs have you done other than being an artist?

Artist: huh?

CM: Lifeguard, Soldier, Medic, Nurse, College Professor, Publisher, Parent, Youth Leader, Slam Coach, Organizer...

83

Black Type Poems

Black Type Haiku

Rude woman haiku No. 86

She told me to go
Back, to where I came from but...
I don't like Cleveland

Colin Kaepernick
And Tonya Harding both known
For Taking a knee

The most destructive words
in the English language are.
We come in peace.

Christopher Michael

.

Black Type Poems

Black Type Poems

Christopher Michael

Black Type Poems

Blacks
Relive
Nightmares

In
This

Dominated
White
Nation

Christopher Michael

Cupids Forgotten

What if police were cupids in a past life?

They mistake pistols for arrows,

desperately trying to help black men find

eternal

love?

Christopher Michael

Black Type Poems

Hashtags & Halos

George Floyd the usual suspect
killed for maybe a fake dollar or check
proof life is not what they respect.
Who's next to get a knee in the neck.

Black ball player black balled taking a knee.
Black man loses life when cops take a knee.
I can't breathe... mama
I don't wanna be another hashtag or halo. (Young boy)

How can one soar to success when they clip the wings
of James Byrd's with Jasper City draggings?

We can't go jogging without buck shots to the belly

They made a meal of Tamir Rice,
seasoned with hashtags and halos
sprinkled with bullets smothered and sautéed bloody
bodies over BB guns in the park.
Like the ones Rakia Boyd caught

the only probable cause is systemic racism

a new video every week.
When they can't pull us out the car in the streets
they deliver hashtags and halos to our couch.
No knock means no right to fight back even when they
get the wrong house.

Black women ain't safe behind closed doors,
when the name on the bullet looks like yours...
Brianna,
Taylor made excuses for every murder.

She looked suspicious
She fit the description
She was resistin'

We sweeten salty tears
With a Sandra Bland hashtag
another tragedy to follow
another suspicious death to swallow.

93

Christopher Michael

It's like they hungry for more hashtags and halos.

King brought us peace and they killed him.

Our people Pulled themselves up by the bootstraps and they bombed them.

Built our own churches and they burned them.

They don't see color.
And
We don't see justice.

They riot when their team wins.
We riot when they slaughter kin
How can you compare that?

I don't want the flame to catch
but we be barrel of black powder they be lit match.

I believe in peace I don't wanna see my city burn.
But we have a right to defend ourselves and
we've run out of cheeks to turn.

No more hashtags
No more halos.

No more hashtags.
No more halos.

Miranda's Warning

Good Day Sir,

I know you're used to talking to family and friends on the other side of glass, but please roll down your window.

Much obliged.

My name is Officer Overseer, I'm with the wish a nigga would county police.

Do you know why you've been stopped, sir?

Well, you look like you're in the wrong neighborhood boy. What plantation you from? Cause, you fit the description of every other North American nigger. I figure right about now you wish world wildlife had you on the endangered species list.

I'm gonna need to see your license, proof of insurance, pass or freedom papers. Let's validate the legality of your presence on this soil, make sure you're on the right side of the invisible line.

Do you mind if I search your vehicle? That was rhetorical, step out of the car boy.

Other than your pigment, do you have anything on you that can hurt me? Maybe a mirror, sharp wit, aggressive attitude, blunt truth, a dime bag of accountability?

Put the camera down, turn around, slowly. Raise your hands as if in praise and worship what time you have left, surrender yourself to me son, let's keep this Civil. Right?

You have the right to be silent, so don't let that mouth escalator your monkey ass to your maker. I have the right to silence you with a 134 decibels of bang bang in ya back.

95

Christopher Michael

It'll be a Glock loaded and locked like a ske-le-ton key to your coffin.

EVERYTHING you say or do will be used against you in the court of my peers, twisted, muted till nothing on this body cam will be able to justify your continued existence.

STOP... RESISTIN!

You have the right to an attorney, crime scene tape, coroner, hashtag and chalk for your outline in case your coon carcass gets out of line.

If you cannot afford an attorney your family can hire one pro-bono to speak to the press, chase indictments and city settlements while I rest on paid administrative leave. When you do this for sport with impunity, you can dodge civil and criminal court with qualified immunity. *I hope you prepicked the pastor for your eulogy.*

Do you understand these wrongs,
as they have been inflicted on you?

Nice,
now do you want the noose
or the knee?

(That one time Nate Sr. asked me to write about something)

Knees & Necks

necks

necks get checked

necks necromance and dance

necks necromance with knees while mommas plead on knees

necks necromance with knees the new noose the roots for strange fruits.

necks necromance with knees the new noose knots hungry for black body rot

necks necromance with knees the new noose knots and negates the next breath

necks necromance with knees the new noose knots and negates noise, that would've pierced the hearts of the blue boys. Voice buried between concrete and polyester blends.

necks necromance with knees the new noose knots and negates noise now, we march? Protest signs always lack the thunder of barking dogs, tear gas, rubber bullets, tasers and white tears. If they can see yo' ass in a crowd, then your skin is too damn loud.

necks necromance with knees the new noose knots and negates noise now no one stops the next one. Extermination requires the annihilation of the entire population.

necks necromance with knees the new noose knots and negates noise <u>now</u> <u>no</u> noose goes UN   filled.   First they came for me, next they'll find a noose for you.

97

Christopher Michael

necks necromance with knees the new noose knots and
negates noise now no noose needed, it's open season. In
your car. On a jog. In your bed.

Don't ask them for help.

necks necromance with knees the new noose knots and
negates noise now no noose needed, knee to grass instead
of foot in ass, respectful protest fails. Divinity says love
your enemy. Violence not solution unless needed for
manifest destiny.

necks necromance with knees the new noose knots and
negates noise now no noose needed, knee necromances
rope, like it loves us. Death becomes us, no justice for us.

necks necromance with knees the new noose knots and
negates noise

now

no

noose

needed

<u>knee</u> necromances necks trying to keep us in check.

necks necromance with knees the new noose knots and
negates noise, now no noose needed,
<u>knee</u> necromances necks
of niggas.

Vampires

They are one of the many examples of the living dead.
Unable to subsist on what Elohim has provided. Sharp
teeth buried in necks sucking the life out of life, out of love.

Fangs fiending for crimson colored con-caved concoctions,
consuming cause they can't create. They appropriate what
flows so natural through the living limbs of the lambs of
God.

Like Leeches or maybe mosquitos bleeding you dry to feed
their young.

They possess a body, they are a body of beings unable to
manifest anything but death, decay and destruction.

Legend says they can transform themselves into creatures
of the night like bats. Can't see the truth but always
talking, flooding the air with noise so they can find their
way. They transform into wolves preying on the weak,
hunting, stalking to devour the innocent.

Fangs loaded into semi-automatic mouths, bullets ready to
pierce the flesh of whoever they've been told to hate that
week.

They descend on the temples of god: Emanual African
Methodist, First Baptist Church of Sutherland Springs.

They descend on the temples of education: Columbine,
Parkland

They descend on the temples of capitalism: Walmart, Pulse.
Do vampires have a pulse?

Ever notice how they avoid the sun lest they burn?

Avoid the light.

99

Christopher Michael

Avoid the truth.

Skin stays pale.

Ever notice how skin

always

white.

black bodies
eat bullets
in bed
before breakfast
and get blamed
for the blood
on the sheets.

Christopher Michael

Black Type Poems

Frailty of Heroes

They stand on pedestals examples of the greatness we can achieve.
They are the echo of ancestors screaming for us to be...
better.
They are greatness personified
all that we can be realized.

Haiku

She wanted him to
be more man like MLK.
So, he phuq'd around

COINTELPRO proved King was no god,
just a man,
tapped that line and listened in on his daydream tapping
the wrong assets.

We worship idols standing on unsteady podiums I bet they
didn't ask to be on,
tip toeing in a field of explosive eggshells navigating their
human
around the wrong move that will cancel them back to
obscurity.

Never meet your real-life hero
for they are just fictional characters.

Those you follow are as flawed,
frail and fallible as you!
These people ain't perfect so there's hope for you

Look at the humans we elevate!
Why should your downfalls stop you from rising?
You too can be great!

Christopher Michael

Haiku

Billie Holiday
Shot up the recording charts
Into her left arm

The irony of needle in black woman taking her life
like needle on black wax still giving us life.

All the melodies she injected
yet we still honor her.

Persons are made of humans
and that's the worst ingredient you can put in people,
they are not ideal idol material.

Let them be examples.
Like them.
But be like you.

Cause no one can do you
better than you
and we need more you.

On the flip side
Our black children are more like our heroes than we
realize,
demoralized,
ostracized,
outcast and assassinated.

Haiku

She wanted son to
Be more man like Malcolm X.
Do you mean, murdered?

If whiteness be the currency,
then blackness be the gold
that gives it value.

Christopher Michael

Black Type Poems

Stuck in Old Glory

🎵 *Oh, I wish I was in the land of cotton,*
Old times there are not forgotten,
Look away, look away, look away Dixie Land. 🎵

America's sins are inseparable from its success.
Ingrained like pain in migraine.
Asked a white friend to open the aspirin,
And hand me some
cause I'll be damn if I ever pick cotton in front of him.

🎵 *Oh, I wish I was in the land of cotton,*

They'll convince you they've forgotten.
They'll want you to stop living in the past
While they're trying to make the south rise again
Taking up residence in days gone by
like their time machine is stuck on old glory
and second place trophies

🎵 *cause Old times there are not forgotten,*

By no one
but the those spawned from the beneficiaries of
compulsory servitude.

🎵 *Look away, look away*

Been looking away for as many years as tears shed
like the sight of the aftermath is too much,
too high to count.
Call that new math
It's common to their core.

🎵 *look away, look away dixie land*

Dixie is always looking for a place to land

107

Christopher Michael

a tradition of colonizers landing on something that don't
belong to them
like Plymouth,
like the back yards of indigenous people,
like the backs of blacks who be the rock.
Our lives,
our ancestors,
their blood,
and all their possibilities
be the immutable foundation of this nation
you can't escape us
cause we be the ball and chain tied to your guilt.
We be the fertilized stench of the privilege you flower in.
You love to blossom
but hate the dirt on your hands.

Warning to neighboring nations: hide your oil, minerals,
people and precious metals cause they'll land on that too.
Liberty is too expensive to maintain without cheap labor
and stolen resources. Just cause I love it here don't mean I
can't smell the truth burning our path to greatness.

Oh, I wish I was in the land of cotton,
As if you could escape it

Old times there are not forgotten,
Your soul will always remember

Look away, look away, look away
Or the mirror will remind you

Dixie Land!

What food, drink, song inspires you?

Artist: I am inspired by all manifestations of the universe's interpretation of itself. To include the consumption of food stuff, mathematically rhythmic vibrations and the animated collection of atomic particles that independently contribute with the individuality they have been blessed with.

Christopher Michael: PB&J

Black Type Poems

Reflective Type Haiku

Cereal Killer
But the milk keeps fighting back
lactose intolerant

If surrounded by
assholes You're probably the
shit in the middle

Christopher Michael

Black Type Poems

Reflective Type Poems

Christopher Michael

Black Type Poems

i feel fine? or "lexa prose" or "prose act"

I wrote this poem where I ask a bunch of questions
about my feelings
or maybe my psychiatric situation
or the result of my chemical balances
that don't see saw
They just depress
or sink
I avoid places with people
I call it Lexaprose or prose act
I ask questions like

and what happens when your feelings flat line
when your fancy fizzles
when all you feel is blank page
hollowed out hole
empty room
when you've got no notion of nothing

is this peace

is this the calm

The poem then moves into these metaphors still asking
questions like

don't storms follow the calm
hunt it down like empty stomach lion hungry for prey
is being centered just standing in the eye of the storm
are you scared of the hail and rain

I think that transition is kinda dope or really good or
adequate enough to convince me to ask myself more
questions like

remember when your heart was a mountain of emotions
is it now flat desert plain
a landscape devoid of skyline

115

what happens when you can't see what you've built

did you think your problems were Holiday Parade Macy's
day floats
like they were easily identified cartoon characters in your
head
what happens when folks
don't care enough to line your streets and enjoy the sights
broadcast news them,
give a damn about them
did you think your mental health was the elephant in the
room
did it hurt more knowing it was just a deflated balloon

Don't miss these similes cause I'm not done

do you feel like flat tire
worn out tread finding it hard to get a grip
do you perceive self as soiled hands
attached to empty cup
didn't you beg for change

Dope right?

did it not help when your cardiac was chemically castrated
are the reuptake inhibitors inhibiting your inhibition
or just your appreciation for improvement,
is professional reassurance of enrichment appearing as
empty promise
are you not aware of your percentage of responsibility
did you confuse insurance with assurance
is this not the upgrade you co-paid for

I love this line!!
did you confuse insurance with assurance
is this not the upgrade you co-paid for

Wait, there's more.

what happens when you still feel abandoned lot,
vacant home,
a derelict adrift
are you ghost ship or
are you more questions than answers

when you feel like open ended sentence
what happens when you feel like that
are you a confused loop
looping on confusion
bewildered as it bends around your doubt
perplexing you as it encircles your uncertainty

do you offer the response you always give when asked

submit unto them your go to line

do you just smile and say,

"I'm fine"

And that's how I end the poem cause,

I'm fine

Christopher Michael

Black Type Poems

Parent O'clock

Alarm
Snooze
Alarm
Stretch
Limbs
Creek
Crack
Iron
His
Mine
Bacon
Eggs
Toast
Love
Bless
Shower
Dress
Dress

Heaven rained down blessings for me to be this happy and
proud of my child.
You've charged me with a life you made me dad.

I wonder if apple trees hurt when the fruit snaps away.
If fruit falls, far from the tree,
who's responsible for the bruises?

Today is the day of days,
their time is up they've worked so hard on this project.

Like clockwork
I put on my blindfold of faith and trust
and release him into the world.

Today God is the cradle.
Yellow chariot arrives to carry him off.

119

I hope he's prosperous
I pray he's Safe

I'm So Dope

Being of sound mind and judgement, I accept
the "I'm so dope challenge"

BEGIN

You can come for me
but you can't afford this hit.
I'm pure dope,
you're cut and mixed
you ain't shit
more like crack,
a fracture,
a fraction,
I'm the denominator
and the numerator,
old school with my craft
you're that common core math.

My pen's too heavy
it'll break your hand every time
like it cracked
a fracture,
a hairline.

Watch how I weave these lines to ya scalp
that's a hair line.
I've been killing it so long
I don't even need a hairline
I'm doper than a razor's edge
I could help you with your hairline
I'm dope like hair glue
these lines will stick to you.

I'm so dope
the cartel's been trying to cut package and sell me.
Smuggle my lines
across imaginary lines like coyotes.

121

Christopher Michael

Transport my poems over the border.
They tried to Peep your poems
and just got boarder.

You might be the latest
but I'm the greatest
I'm Dope
like Ali against the ropes
you'll wear yourself out swinging for me.
Stop reaching for me
@mrmichael310
you'd do good to just follow me.
I'm nutritious and delicious
I'll detox that ass
that's why ya girl keeps swallowing me.

She likes how I tickle and tantalize that top hole those
thighs this thing ain't tame it's trained she ain't even
fightin' I'm so dope I'm a Tongue Titan!

I'm so dope
I don't have time
to memorize
I'm dope like essential
Thank GOD I got these nurse credentials.

Writing this was a nice vacation
you'd be safer practicing social isolation
You in the wrong room
at the wrong party where's your invitation
Your immune system ain't strong enough to leave the
house yet better get that vaccination

I swear I wear a mask to protect you,
my spits that sick.
I'm dope like COVID
I shut down shit.

King Crastinate

Call me King crastinate
I precrastinate,
as well as I postcrastinate
I'm a pro.

I am a procrastinatic genius.
I mean I'm good under pressure.
I mean the good ideas don't even start till the clock's about
to run out.
I pull brilliance out my ass like a rabbit magicianed out a
hat.

Not sure if being good at crunch is compensation for
always waiting till the last minute but I need the pressure
to Diamond out the best ideas.

Stop asking me if I have a plan
 I'll figure it out as I go along.

Touched by God to improv through life.
I don't know what's next
so ride
or get left.

(note to self: finish this poem tomorrow)

123

Christopher Michael

Black Type Poems

Kirk

I wrote my paper on the most important man of my formative years. He was there when mom was grinding hustle into food, leasing her time to keep the lights lit, offered up her dreams as sacrifice for a roof, endured corporate clowns constantly trying to Caucasian the culture from her hair and clothes so I could Christmas.

A military man who taught me how to lead and command. He taught me selfless service so I could hindsight all that my mother has ever done. His weekly example taught me cunning ingenuity, perseverance and work. My only example of manhood, ladies and gentlemen James Tiberius Kirk. Captain, Enterprise, NC1701, Earth.

He was that man that commanded the 5-year mission to boldly go where his family couldn't. Like my dad on his 5 year, 10 year, 15 year, I was 15 when I met him.

That's cool Cause Kirk gave me the courage to explore the universe of my feelings. Taught me how to love a woman but not how to keep one, still learning how to lower my Shields before I beam her aboard.

Young me the primitive civilization, dad the Star fleet officer refusing to interfere with my development like it was his prime directive. Had Never met him, to miss him, assumed he was a redshirt that didn't make it back from an away mission. An absent honor chasing warrior while I had my mom to Klingon.

Kirk was always there with me, a child of the latch key he taught me to do what's right even if it meant breaking a rule or two. He and uncle Spock taught, the needs of the many outweight the needs of the few even if you find you've fallen on the side of the few, but will still risk it all cause we don't leave anyone behind.

125

Captain Kirk's bond with uncle Spock and uncle McCoy showed me the joy of openly loving friends like John, Dominique, Richard, Robert, Kevin, Joe B., Jomar, Ed, Allen, Brian, Chris and both Brandon's without the fear I'd have to abandon, my, me. That there is love in masculinity and manhood can be beautiful and that my momma was all I needed, she was the Star in my Trek

FOOTNOTE: Turns out my dad was ok after all. He was being held captive by a hostile force and is now retired from Starfleet. He knew The Captain as well as I do and he's glad I had him.

Snooty Too

They call me snootysmoothpenz. I come from a long line of creative genius. You [laugh] well you come from a short line of cliche lines.

My mother was Maya Angelou and father was Dr. Seuss. Your daddy must have been a part time thrash man and remedial math teacher which explains why that garbage you spit don't add up.

You're not even half the poet I am. You're a mongrel, Mughal, mutt ass poet. Which explains why you're just a half ass poet.

No... We cannot be friends on my Facebook page. No, you are not fly enough to share my stage. Your poem would be greatly improved if you just spit on the page. By that I mean hock a loogie on your poem, smear the ink into an abstract blur THEN I might pay attention. "I think the artiste was attempting to illustrate the plight of the slammist among a sea of WHACK ASS POETS."

This may come off as arrogance, but I don't win slams by chance. Their side conversations when you spit is the proof that my opinion of you is the truth.

I am that... Superman type poet and my only kryptonite is you whack ass poet, ass poet. Phuqin phuqin... You make me twitch ass poets like I got Tourette's BITCH ass poet.

I'm that why should I burn precious calories giving you claps here's two snaps ass poet.

Sorry I'm too busy practicing my own ish so no I didn't hear you spit ass poet.

I am that... Hottest poet in the nation but few people know cause I'm too busy with a family and a real job ass poet. No!

Christopher Michael

You are not my peer, you're flipping fries I'm flipping careers.

Yes, I check Facebook every ten minutes to make sure folks are still talking about me. I'm that worthy of the center of attention ass poet.

I roll with a poet that has more metaphors in her menses meaning, her flow is funkier than yours. You're barely filling sheets she's filling pads she's a bad ass poet... PERIOD! You might wanna call the Doc.

Medium ball points are bolder so I only wrap my fingers around Queen Pens. I'm silkysmoothpenz the original snootysmoothpenz. This is where the bourgeoisie poetry begins.

I blaze joints. I'm the bastard that does it for the points. I write for reaction. I pimp poetry for the spotlight that's right I write for the attention.

And every one of you secretly confesses to yourself at night... Christopher Michael is the baddest metaphor to rock the mic.

I'm welcome, now thank me very much.

Cluster Phuq

It feels... world ending.
It feels... like the end of existence.
Imagine the universe in the hands of a maniacal god whose
bending it in the wrong direction just to hear its scream of
pain and I feel all of it,
concentrated on one temple,
behind one eye.
I'm talking grown man cry
through the pain
with no shame.

It's a red-hot, iron crowbar, slowly trying to pry out my
eye.
My face the lost ark,
the devil itself trying to raid it.
What treasure could I be hiding?
He's Breaking through my window Pain,
there's got to be an easier way to steal my soul.

Head in vice, like dog in bear trap, wish I could gnaw off my
face.
Desperate to escape,
this is every day,
fear of the next attack leaves me depressed in this place.

So far, all the chemical concoctions created to correct this
curse cause my blood pressure to ascend leaving me with...
ANOTHER PHUQing HEADACHE!

Even when it's gone it shadows me,
constantly reminding me,
it's always coming.
It's always lurking around the corner.
My personalized trigger warning,
ever so slightly tapping my temple a demon scratching at
the door,
but wait there's more.

129

I dream in pain, HiFi, Dolby, THX

Before I'm aware enough, before I can climb out of the sleep
I just fell in, the pain invades my dreams. I dream in pain,
like you dream in color or cartoon or black and white. The
pain alarm clocks its way around my skull with no snooze,
I may never again sleep. It's embarrassing the way I plead
to a God who's clearly got his phone on airplane mode.

These headaches Cluster around my clock twice a day
damn near every day I can set my watch to their drum
beating me into submission.

It aches, it throbs, it burns, it radiates like a slow-moving
bolt of lightning burning from temple to brow to eye to
teeth.

Imagine all the pain of your 5-day vomit inducing migraine
concentrated into 60 minutes. You get to eat the elephant
bite by bite but I have to swallow it whole.

10 out of 10 pain scale is for the privileged.

I wish it was a 10.

10 is where I begin.

Phuq a 10 I want peace.

I want sleep.

I Am Nurse

During my
formative,
figure out what I want to be that I will enjoy
AND be lucrative but not really considering the financial
ramifications in the form of government backed loan shark
loans years.

I considered being a Biogenetic Engineer,
learn how to splice some genes and get me some
superpowers.

Or maybe a cardiothoracic surgeon cause that sounds like
an unnecessarily complicated job title.

I knew I wanted to be close to some Star Trek level science
like

half warrior
half miracle worker
all explorer.

Turns out the Army had what I was looking for.

Some people work for a living.
I work to keep you living.

I serve. I Save. I shelter when sick.
I am your sword and shield.

I've been instructed, trained and educated.
Certified, Licensed and Registered.
I am teacher. I am caretaker. I am soldier. I am nurse.

I am the foundation of care, I do it all.
I'm the Swiss Army knife of medical professionals.
With God above me there is no task beneath me.

Christopher Michael

no metaphor in this meaning when I say I will put up with your crap,
wipe you clean when your world has wavered.
Brush your teeth, comb your hair, shave your face, or wash your nasty...

OFTEN,

too busy to pee
bladder like a camel I hump these pills from room to room.
12-hour shifts
we don't get to sit
you'd think my feet were in love
The way my arches have fallen for you

CARING when no one else will.
Epic levels of empathy.
Knowing what you need before you do.
Protecting your privacy.
Teaching wet behind the ears docs.
Fighting through fatigue,
muscling through migraines to perform in pain.
I show up!!

But ain't that what superheroes do? When you have a cape tucked under your scrubs there's too little room for humility. So... You're welcome and thank me very much.

When the sanctum of your soul suffers Benedict betrayal,
attacked by arthritis,
cursed with cancer
I am your comforter.

When your family falters
I'll be by your side.

When your poor choices
leave your body a bruised, bloody, battered battle ground
of regret.
When you become a field of foreign invaders

I will hold your hand through the fight.

I braved Ebola.
I hung in with hugs for HIV.
I survived the swine flu
And now I'm a certified black belt in COVID Karate

When baby Mobley was admitted for failure to thrive
abandoned by his mother
I worked 16-hour days to literally love him back to life.

One time I had to tell an inmate, the biggest as...
(I mean a troubled young man with behavioral issues) that
his immune system was inadequate to combat the
deficiency he acquired. Most assuredly he brought it on
himself.

He was a pain in my side
but it didn't affect my give a damn,
I even advocate for the as...
troubled young men with behavioral issues

It's a skill to set aside learned behavior, cultural beliefs,
prejudices and political affiliations to love a person in need.
I'm not judging you; I'm clinically assessing you. I see that
rebel flag tattoo, but I will not allow that to effect how I
care for you.

I'm cultured in Christianity,
but conversion of religion is not my mission,
so the compassion and cuisine will be Kosher.
I will make sure you know the direction of Mecca
While working around all five of your prayer times
I will advocate while you meditate.
I **Can't** get you unlimited lives,

but I can point to the power ups.

Help you with the HEALTH meter.

133

Christopher Michael

Teach you cheat codes for the game of life.
And if your body fails the test
I will bring you dignity in death

In such high demand,
Nursing Schools can't crank us out fast enough.
Do you know compassion?
Ok with a little blood?
Well, we need you.

Our life is love
Our job is care
We are nurse

PB&J

It has a magical medicinal power
to put my parts back to restart.
Protein, carbs and sugar.
The nut, the wheat and the grape.
Halts my headaches,
crushes my cranky
and tantalizes my tongue.
The key to which reinstalls a happy belly.
All hail the sandwich,
Peanut Butter & Jelly.

******

Writing prompt: Food
From: Thembi Min Clubhouse
Poetry Palace 01.08.21

Christopher Michael

Black Type Poems

Dear Chin,

It has come to my attention that you are concerned with
my feelings about you.
That you worry that you are my least favorite body part.
As a matter of fact, I do love you, like you, sorta.
I don't keep you covered because you're too round and I
prefer that chiseled jaw look.
I don't cover you because you give my head an overall
shape that makes me mmmmm... regret my reflection.

I cover you because you're the perfect foundation.
You're the soil for generous growth.
You're the BASE of follicular operations.
Besides chin,
who has earned the right to your magnificent modesty?
Do you not enjoy the warmth of beard on winter's nights?
Do you not relish the dew from pores gliding down
platinum shafts catching the breeze on a Texas summer
chilling you to satisfaction?

Do you not?

I really find your lack of appreciation for all I've done for
you disturbing.
You're an essential ornation for my mandibular
magnificence, must we discuss this further friend?
You know who really loves you?
Hand!
Righty is always raving at how well you rest on fist when
brain is deep in thought.
You two always get along so well.

I don't just love you, well like you, not really but I
KNEEEED you.
That's right knees.
You don't hear them complaining when I cover them with
pants!
SHUT UP PENIS IT'S THE LAW! Wait till we get home.

137

Christopher Michael

Chin, chin, chiiiin, stop trying to cry you LOOK silly.
Cause I need them to see with!
That's their job I can't cover them up.
Look! Look! Look!
This is ridiculous,
you had your time to shine when we were in the army.
Roles have changed.
Life ain't fair.

I'm done with this conversation.

Shout out to Write About Now, Christopher Diaz and Pages Matam for the writing prompt.

The Truth Inn Us

I got them all fooled into thinking *I'm For Public
Consumption.* Disguised as *Creativity,* and fooled by my
Ink, been keeping my feelings caged, solitary confinement,
no profit like *Prison Industrial Complex.* No one gets in the
Door.

Not *Just A Book* easily read, so I keep my words spoken
and my heart *Blindfolded,* avoiding more scratches in my
groove It's *Just a Vinyl Record* wax that can't handle more
heat than a well temperatured room. I need this thing to
last me a few more years.

Been trying to protect you since the day *I Met You.*

Lost track of how many times you helped me with my Ink I
think *You Smell Like* the rocket fuel of my success. *The
Most Beautiful* part of my growth my *Favorite* friend you
are my superpower.

I STILL keep this cardiac caged cause.
I *Don't Beg* for better,
but it shows up anyway.
I guess,
I'm *Just Blessed.*

Christopher Michael

Black Type Poems

What do you dislike about the art world?

Artist: I love all individual manifestations of creation, everything in this world positive or negative can be used to inspire the next great work. There is no dislike in my heart.

Christopher Michael: Pretentious answers to simple questions and anyone uttering the phrase "that's what poetry is truly about"

Black Type Poems

We are the created creating creation.

www.mrmichael310.com
@mrmichael310
@310brownstreet

Made in the USA
Monee, IL
27 September 2021

d3a2ddf6-8280-4522-abbe-d11b3b2a2808R01